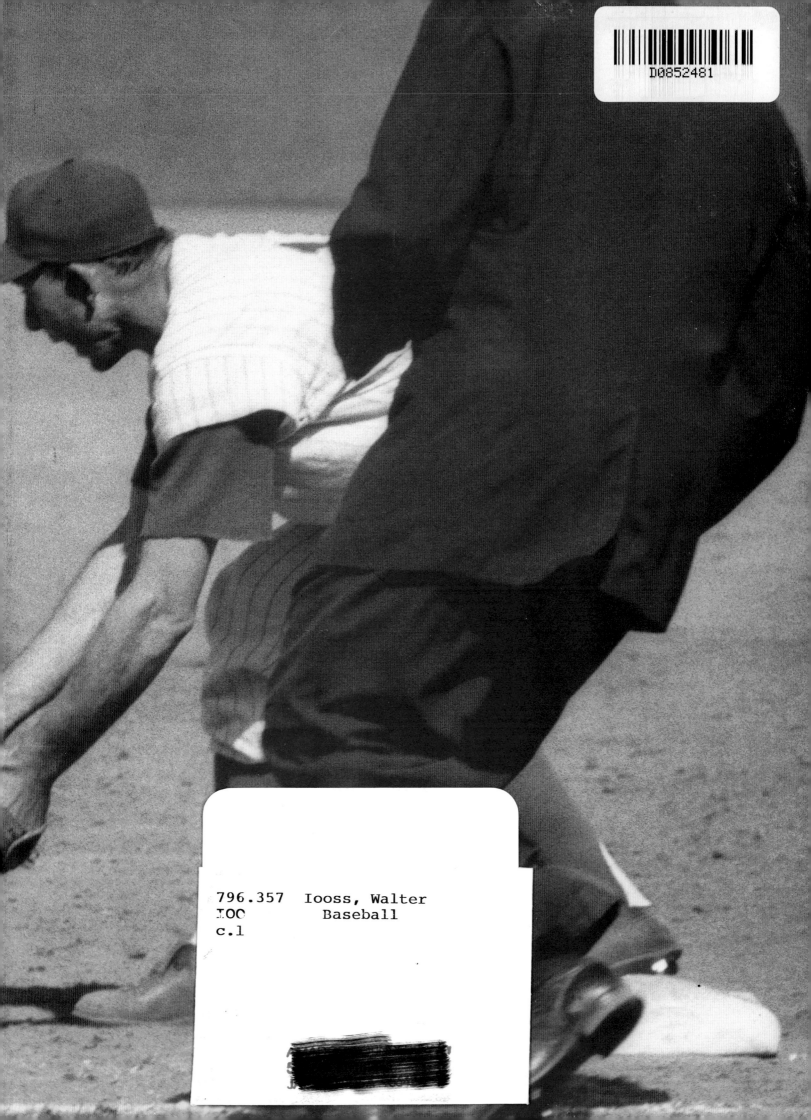

	1	2	3
DET	0	0	2
BOSTON	1	0	2

BAT   BALL

Photographs by Walter Iooss, Jr.

Text by Roger Angell

Harry N. Abrams, Inc., Publishers, New York

To My Father

———Walter Iooss, Jr.

Project Director: Robert Morton
Designer: Dirk Luykx

Third Printing, 1985

On the preceding pages:
Endpapers: R.L. Miller and Gil Hodges. Polo Grounds, New York, September 1963
Page 1: Home Run. Reggie Jackson, Yankee Stadium, New York, August 1980
Pages 2–3: First Inning. County Stadium, Milwaukee, June 1979
Pages 4–5: Pre-game Warmup. Jarry Park, Montreal, July 1969
Pages 6–7: Joe Morgan and Mickey Rivers. Riverfront Stadium, Cincinnati, World Series 1976
Pages 8–9: Roberto Clemente. Three Rivers Stadium, Pittsburgh, June 1970
Pages 10–11: Dick Allen. Connie Mack Stadium, Philadelphia, August 1969
Pages 12–13: Jim Rice. Fenway Park, Boston, August 1978
Pages 14–15: World Series—Oakland vs. Cincinnati. Oakland-Alameda Stadium, Oakland, October 1972
Page 16: Willie Mays. Polo Grounds, September 1963

Library of Congress Cataloging in Publication Data
Iooss, Walter, Jr.
    Baseball.
Summary: Color photographs of great moments and great
players of the past twenty years in baseball, accompanied
by an essay on the sport and the photographer.
    1. Baseball—Pictorial works. 2. Baseball—Addresses,
essays, lectures. [1. Baseball. 2. Photography of
sports] I. Angell, Roger. II. Title.
GV867.3.I6   1984   796.357′022′2   84-9268
ISBN 0-8109-0711-9

Published in 1984 by Harry N. Abrams, Incorporated, New York

Printed and bound in Japan

Somebody is always trying to improve baseball. A few years ago, a fan sent me an ingenious proposal designed to add variety and zest to the old game by means of one small shift in the rules: a batter who had just struck the ball or who had drawn ball four would have the option of heading for first base *or third base*. If he selected the latter route, he would then be required to proceed around the bases in the same startling clockwise direction, and his ensuing fortunes and adventures along the way would be governed by the existing rules of the game. I regret that I have forgotten the author of this inspired document (it was subsequently published and reprinted in several sporting journals), for his little swerve or jiggle in the straitlaced laws of the pastime offers more possibilities for surprise and entertainment than one might at first suppose. The scheme and its results are still sometimes talked about in dugouts and bullpens around the leagues. Think about it. Let's say that our batsman steps up to the plate with no outs and a teammate on first base, and taps a routine bouncer toward first—a good chance for a double play, you say, except that the batter, exercising his new option, sensibly sprints north instead of south, while the runner at first, now no longer subject to the force play, holds his base. The first baseman, fielding the ball, halts in mid-pivot when he notices that there will be no play at second, then realizes that there will be nothing doing at first base either, and at last gets off his peg to third, far too late for the out. Base hit, runners at first and third; still no outs. As it happens, both these baserunners are quick and each now takes a good lead off his base. The pitcher anxiously throws over to first a couple of times, to keep the runner close, then tries a pickoff at third. No luck. He delivers a strike, then a ball, and on the next pitch both runners take off for second. The pitch is low and away to the right-handed batter, slightly discomposing the catcher; his good peg is a hair late, and both sliding runners are safe out there (a double palms-down gesture by the ump), where they greet each other with double hand-slaps and help dust off each other's pants.

Other possibilities now suggest themselves. If the game were a close one (or even if it *weren't* close, now that I think about it) both men would immediately try to steal the next base, given the absolute guarantee that at least one of them would be safe and now in scoring position. If both were safe, and if the flustered pitcher understandably lost his control for a bit, we might soon find *two* baserunners at each corner. Now what? Now a sacrifice fly to medium-deep center field, please, with the two inbound runners tagging up after the catch and both—arriving at opposite corners of the plate in converging clouds of dust—just beating the throw home ("Ah, there, José" . . . "Can it be you again, *amigo* Dwayne?"), while both outbound men trot along to second on the play. In no time, one can envisage, the bases might be loaded— and I mean *loaded*—and the next man. . . . No, it won't work. The possibilities have begun to outweigh our anticipations, the umpires are overburdened, and pity for the pitcher and the infield defense dims our wish for further wonders—a double rundown between second and third, say, or a six-run triple to deep center, with the concentric circles of baserunners whirling about the base-paths in a double pinwheel of overpopulation and, yes, ennui.

Baseball, we understand once again, is spare and rigorous by nature, and is also somehow *right*. We can ignore it or hate it, if that is our choice, but we must take it as it is. It cannot be better.

Like most fans, I mumble and groan about the great alterations that baseball has undergone in my lifetime. Some of these—the inflation of salaries to undreamed-of levels as an aftermath of the players' attainment of free agency in the mid-1970s, and the general availability of the sport everywhere via television—have permanently changed the way we watch and think about baseball now. These social alterations are inevitabilities, I suppose, but other invented changes—indoor baseball, artificial turf, the designated hitter device—might have been avoided, for it can be argued (I will argue it at length, but not here) that each of them has done damage to the logic and fabric of the game. But the truth of the matter, of course, is that baseball has hardly changed at all. The game on the field, though played now by young millionaires and watched, idly and imperfectly, by millions of us in our living rooms, is almost exactly the same game that we learned as children, and that our fathers and grandfathers watched when they were children. Most of us went to our first big-league game in the company of a male relative whose memory of past seasons and knowledge of the tactics and subtleties of the game on the field (amazingly revealed, inning by inning, there in the cramped, oddly comfortable seats in stands upsloping from those long and vividly peopled green lawns before us) transformed that day, we almost sensed, from an outing and a treat into something more substantial: into a rite. Distracted by peanuts and strange faces, we needed a little time before noticing that that grown-up beside us seemed to recognize the brief flurries of movement and the alternating lengthy and languid intervals of inaction down there on the field as a continuation of patterns and events he had been carrying with him, all unknown to us, for decades past. The players that he named for us, pointing them out around the diamond or as they stepped up to the plate, were interspersed in his account with the names and feats of their famous predecessors, young ballplayers now old and gone away but still clearly seen in his mind's eye, and still loved or feared, we could suddenly tell, in memory. No other sport is presented and preserved in quite this fashion. No other sport, I am sure, has kept itself so austerely the same. The dimensions of baseball—the weight and size and feel of the ball; the length and composition of the bat; the peculiar geometry of the plate; the elegant distances between the bases; the distance from the mound to the plate (sixty feet, six inches, which exactly permits a curve or slider to move, laterally and vertically, just as it crosses the plate, thus transforming batting from swat to art, the most difficult of all sports skills); the mysterious business of counting balls and strikes, hits and outs, sides and innings to mark the ticking-off of the invisible game-clock (this measurement above all)—are what make the game work the way it does, and none of these has been substantially altered or has needed alteration in this century.

When we add to all this the ingredients of variety and continuity, we step even closer to the center of things. Because pitching matters so much and because there are different pitchers out there every day, the tone and plot of each contest can vary wonderfully from yesterday's game and the one that will be played tomorrow, even when the same two teams are on the field. The Milwaukee Brewers won the opening game of the 1982 World Series in a laugher, beating the Cardinals by 10–0 and crashing seventeen hits to the Cards' three, but lost the next day by 5–4, when a Milwaukee relief pitcher walked in the winning run with the bases loaded. Later on that week, the Brewers needed but one more victory to clinch the Series, but dropped the last two games to the Redbirds by 13–1 and 6–3. This is nearly amazing. If the first game and sixth game of the Series had been played as a double-header, the fans that day would have seen a twenty-two-run swing between the contesting teams. Or, to go back a bit, look at the World Series of 1960, in which the lordly Yankees won three non-successive games from the Pirates, by scores of 16–3, 10–0, and 12–0, but lost the championship because the Pirates beat them in four games, by 6–4, 3–2, 5–2, and, in the seventh-game clincher, 10–9. None of the media-people at either classic marvelled much about these sudden swoops and reversals, for they are a commonplace of the game, observable by anyone who follows the scores and standings for a couple of weeks during the regular season, but one cannot imagine such turnabouts in any other team sport.

Baseball looks easy and, to the uninitiated, insufficiently eventful, but it is implacably difficult and stuffed with surprise, and very few teams or players dominate its fortunes for long. In the middle of August of 1983, the soaring Baltimore Orioles, at the beginning of a streak that brought them fifteen victories in eighteen games and took them to the top of their division for keeps, were stopped in their tracks by the Texas Rangers, thanks to a 2–0, one-hit performance by a semi-anonymous Texas pitcher named John Butcher, who had not started a game since early April. A day or two later, Chuck Rainey, a veteran right-hander with the abysmal Chicago Cubs, startled himself and some careworn Cubbie fans at Wrigley Field by pitching no-hit ball against the Cincinnati Reds for eight and two-thirds innings, before giving up— oh, *no!*—a solid first-pitch single to Eddie Milner, for the Reds' only hit of the afternoon. Terrible luck, of course, but perhaps Rainey's luck (and Butcher's, too) was in coming so close in the first place.

Dave Righetti, the big Yankee left-hander, had already pitched a genuine no-hitter against the Red Sox on July 4th, 1983, and in September Bob Forsch, of the Cardinals, threw a 3–0 no-hitter against the Expos, and then Mike Warren, a twenty-two-year-old Oakland rookie, did the same thing to the White Sox. Forsch's masterpiece was the second no-hit game of his career; his brother, Ken Forsch, now with the Angels, has a 1979 no-hitter to his credit, which makes them the only brothers ever to pull off the double. None of this is entirely surprising, nor should we be struck dumb with wonder by the news that there were no no-hit games at all during the 2,106 major-league encounters played the year before, and that Bob Forsch's and Mike Warren's no-hitters came within three days of each other. "In baseball," Yogi Berra has told us, "you don't know nothing." What we do know, perhaps, is that there is always a large dollop of luck involved when any pitcher, no matter how imperious or crafty, gets by twenty-seven batters without seeing one harmless grounder bounced through the middle or a half-hit flare drop untouched in short right field. That sudden little scattering of no-hit games in 1983 statistically illuminates the same essential attribute of the game.

Perfect games—no hits, no one on base—are much more scarce, of course. Len Barker, of the Cleveland Indians, last turned this trick in 1981, when he retired twenty-seven Blue Jay batters in succession, for the only perfecto in the past fifteen years. Like all fans, I admire remarkable individual performances—a five-for-five day at the plate, forty homers in a summer, two hundred hits in a season, or twenty or more victories by a pitcher—and of course I have memorized the landmark wonders—Ted Williams's .406 batting average in 1941, Don Larsen's perfect game in the 1956 World Series, Bob Gibson's 1.12 earned-run average in 1968, and so forth—but I find more and more that my awe is reserved for the game itself, whose unforgiving difficulty makes prodigious performances, in a game or a season or a career, so rare that when they do come along they light up our imagination and keep alive that wonder that we first brought to this game. The game yields itself (a little) to luck as well as to resolute or brilliant performance, and the proportions of that mixture—a recipe more subtle than the *béarnaise* at La Grenouille—are exquisitely pleasing. If the game were harder, if it only rewarded the Cobbs and Groves and Williamses and Gibsons of the sport, and never the John Butchers and Mike Warrens, we would know the outcome of every game in advance, and we would gossip or read or snooze whenever the bottom of the order was up at bat. If it were all much easier, if there were a no-hitter every week and a grand-slam homer every evening, we would pay no attention until the ninth, for only the score would matter, and the constant surprises of baseball would look only eccentric or else elude us altogether.

Baseball's placid and orderly exterior conceals so many possibilities for the unique circumstance that this, too—a first-ever play or an utterly unexpected series of events—is a commonplace of the sport. Last August, the California Angels, playing a home game against the Minnesota Twins, seemed to have matters comfortably in hand when, already leading by 2–0, they put their first two batters on base in the bottom of the fourth, only to crash headlong into Yogi Berra's dictum. The next California batter, Ron Jackson, hit a low line drive to third baseman Gary Gaetti, who flipped to second to double off the lead baserunner, and in plenty of time for the relay over to first, which beat the other retreating Angel baserunner to the bag. Triple play. The next pitch of the game, delivered by Tommy John to the Twins' Gaetti, now become the leadoff batter in the top of the fifth, was smashed over the fence, and the *next* pitch, to Tom Brunansky, also departed the premises, tying the score in the game, which the Twins eventually won by 4–2. Three successive pitches, good for three outs, two runs, one ruined game, and uncounted broken hearts: according to the records, this had never happened before in major-league baseball. And neither could anyone quite remember an inning like the one that the Orioles came up with a few days later, in a game against the Blue Jays at Baltimore. The Orioles had rallied for two runs in the bottom of the ninth, tying the game at 3–3, but in the process used up their last catcher, who had given way to a pinch hitter—a spendthrift maneuver that now required Baltimore manager Joe Altobelli to send a reserve infielder, Lenn Sakata, out to catch in the tenth. The Blue Jays led off the extra inning with a home run and a single, thus bringing on a new Baltimore pitcher, Tippy Martinez. The Torontos, one may assume, had noted the presence of Sakata behind the plate, and were understandably eager—a bit overeager, in fact—to test him with attempted thefts of second, but they never did find the answer. Martinez instantly picked the baserunner off first. He walked the next man but also picked him off, then surrendered a single, and notched the third out with his third pickoff of the inning. Ah, baseball. No one, I think, was particularly surprised when Sakata won the game, in the bottom of the same inning, with a three-run homer.

The setting of the game matters almost as much as its arduousness and amazements, and baseball's place in the American calendar is unique. Other sports cluster their action on weekends and play sporadically during the rest of the week, as their barnstormers move from city to city around the circuit, playing but a single game at each site and then wearily decamping, almost before we have noticed their presence in town. Baseball, by contrast, is a part of summer, played almost every day from early April to late October, and its onflowing half-heard sounds and news belong as much to our hot-weather afternoons and evenings as do the whine of outboards, the hum of the air conditioner, and the September whir of locusts in heat-heavy trees. It is the sameness and dailiness of baseball—baseball as soap opera—and the next day's resultant boxscores, barely altered standings and statistics, and foolishly refreshed hopes and sharpened anxieties, that confirm both the rarity and sweet familiarity of our old, upspringing keepsake. More people go to big league games now (45,565,910 of them last year) and (I suspect) follow baseball than ever before, and no wonder.

My slighting reference to televised baseball should be explicated before we move along to the baseball photographs by Walter Iooss that make up this book. The argument against television as a proper vehicle for baseball (aside from its general corruption of our attention and its way of making all sports look and seem the same) has to do with the medium's congenital impatience, its need to hurry. Televised baseball—particularly the network presentations—often seems to me to be moving at a faster pace than the game that is being covered: a curious business, to say the least. The silences of baseball and its quality of waiting, both inherent to the pastime, are habitually talked away by the announcers or twitched away by rapid camera cutting. Sitting before my set in mid-game, I try to pay attention to Bill Madlock's batting stance and to pick up how Steve Rogers is pitching to him this time around, or, if the camera eye gives us that news, how the infield is deployed, but just bringing me these useful sights is not enough for the people doing the game, for they must bury them in a running tide of accompanying commentary and sidelight, preview and gossip. The count to Madlock goes to two and two, and, since this is a network game, my excellent view of him standing in for the next pitch, with his dangerous bat raised behind his ear, is suddenly joined by a smaller, set-in image of Madlock on the screen—a head-shot of him being interviewed before this game has begun and talking about his Pirates' chances in the remaining weeks of the pennant race, or perhaps by a similar shot of Madlock's manager, Chuck Tanner, telling us what a steadying and inspiriting presence Bill has been to his younger Pirate teammates this summer. The moment—Madlock at the plate, Rogers on the mound, two Pirates leading away from their bases—has been blunted, and almost without knowing it we have become a bit indifferent to it, a little impatient with the matter at hand. Television by habit makes us want the *next* action, the next (or the past) piece of news, with no intervening few beats of silence; it urges us to stay tuned at every instant—don't touch that set!— but urges this so often and with such insistence that we can't stay tuned where it matters, which is in our heads. We cannot stop and taste what we have before us, for the proprietors of this show and this medium are afraid that they will lose us if we do. They may be right about this, I think, if we are watching police cars or a talk show or basketball, but they are wrong about baseball, which is a game, as Bill Veeck has pointed out, that is meant to be savored.

The televising of baseball has improved steadily in the past few years, and its cameras and expert announcers can teach us more about pitching than is ever visible from the stands, but I don't think it will ever be entirely comfortable with this old game, which does not need its time nudged along (as outsiders to the sport always seem to think) or its anticipation honed by talk, but rather invites us really to go slow, for a change, almost to stop, in order to reflect on what is before us and what is to come. It has occurred to me more than once that baseball and reading have a good deal in common, for there is time in both pastimes for the considering pause, for a thoughtful glance backward (this is why we learn to keep score), and for slowly rising and enveloping expectations. Readers and baseball fans are not much bothered by tedious early chapters, for these are preamble to the rewards that can arrive later in the day.

Baseball, as we all know, does have its share of dreary or terrible ballgames—a chilly, early-season evening encounter between two noncontending clubs that produces a thin procession of popups and infield outs interspersed with an occasional three-bounce single and in time (clap, clap) a run or two; or an elephantine Sunday afternoon burlesque, bulging with home runs and mistakes, successive bases on balls, missed cutoff men, a fight in the stands, a sure double-play messed up, an *intentional* base on balls, slow strolls to the mound by the coaches and managers, repeated cart-trips from the bullpen, irritable waves of pointless cheering, a between-the-wickets infield error, a pinch-hitter batting in place of another pinch-hitter, your increasingly illegible scorecard, a long *long* drive that goes foul at the last instant, the feeling of trampled popcorn underfoot, derisive cheers, a bases-empty two-out base on balls, and the wrong team (I *knew* it) at last winning the thing by five runs. But the next game—the one that comes along the next evening, or on your next visit to the park—is the one that makes up for it all, for it sticks in memory and flowers there.

If we think about a taut, well-played game that we have just seen (or a rousing series, or even part of a season sometimes) it seems to break down into stopped moments, to be looked at and played over in recollection because so much happened in that instant, and because so much led up to it and grew out of it. Without recourse to my scorebook or to the *Baseball Guide,* I can still bring back the top of the seventh inning of the sixth game of the wonderful World Series of 1979, between the Pirates and the Orioles, when some minute trifles of strategy and circumstance determined the larger course of events, as they so often do. Baltimore manager Earl Weaver had stationed his first baseman, Eddie Murray, close to the baseline against the leadoff Pittsburgh batter, Omar Moreno—a routine defensive precaution against a left-handed batter late in a close game (it was scoreless, in fact), when a sharply pulled drive up the line might wind up in the right-field corner for a double or worse. Routine but perhaps misguided, for the Baltimore pitcher, Jim Palmer, was not and is not accustomed to surrendering pulled line shots to singles hitters like Moreno (thanks to his superb control, he has never given up a grand-slam home run in his four thousand-odd major-league innings pitched), and Palmer, unhappily kicking the mound out there, was clearly not in agreement with his skipper. A moment later, Moreno hit a hopping little grounder that, sure enough, just eluded Murray's dive to his right—a single. Moreno, a very fast baserunner, next set sail for second on a hit-and-run play, and the batter, Tim Foli, struck a chopper over the mound that Palmer, leaping, touched with his glove but could not hold; the minute deflection caused the Baltimore shortstop to misplay the ball slightly, in front of second base, and all hands were safe. If Palmer had caught the bouncer, or if he had missed it altogether, or if Weaver had allowed Eddie Murray to station himself at a normal remove from first base, the bases in all likelihood would now be empty and the Pirates down to their last out of the inning—ifs and buts of some import, since the next batter, Dave Parker, thus given his chance, now hit a rocket that suddenly seemed to dive under the second-baseman's glove and on into center field, scoring Moreno and breaking open the critical game, which the Pirates won, 4–0, thereby positioning themselves for their world championship victory the next afternoon.

Television, I think we can agree, is temperamentally unsuited to this sort of archaeology; the twenty-minute, rather than the instant, replay is sometimes wanted, for the game's own scholarly pace and recapitulative energy wonderfully reward and sustain its patient fans. It is not surprising that there has been such a flow of good baseball books and lively baseball publications in recent years—almost a flood of them now—and that contemporary statisticians and historians have been finding new ways to tell us what is really going on out there. The game is at once linear and mathematical; one thing happens and then another and another, and almost every event or accident on the field also becomes a number—ball or strike, hit or error, out or run—and then a statistic. There is time to write it all down and to figure it out and try to get it right—which is as close as most of us will ever come to hitting the ball to the first-base side of the infield with a man on second or striking out the last batter with an in-running fastball. Nowadays, if you so wish, you can put your hands on *Day by Day in Cleveland Indians History*; or read a first-class biography of Casey Stengel (*Stengel—His Life and Times*, by Robert Creamer); or immerse yourself in a hilarious anthology of quotations about the game by hundreds of the people who have played it or worked in it (*Voices of Baseball*, Bob Chieger) or buy and study the Milwaukee Brewers' own players' instructional manual; or subscribe to *The Minneapolis Review of Baseball* or *The Sports Collector's Digest* (which is ninety percent baseball); or, going a bit deeper, join the Society for American Baseball Research, in Cooperstown, N.Y., which will list you and your address and your particular baseball passions (The Negro Leagues, say, or Hall of Fame pitchers before 1930, or Terre Haute-born major-leaguers, or the Red Stockings of 1871–75, or whatever) in their next directory of more than two thousand members, and also mail you the society's estimable periodicals, wherein you can learn, for instance, that Carl Yastrzemski hit more home runs after reaching the age of forty than anyone else, or that Lou Gehrig stole home fifteen times—I can't get *over* it—in his career, while Lou Brock only did it once. Or, if numbers really light you up, you can buy the annual *Baseball Abstract*, by Bill James, a demon diamond statistician who has invented the art of Sabermetrics (acronymically honoring the aforementioned Society), which extends baseball's everyday stats into new formulas and theorems and entire cloudy continents of player evaluation and game theory: the Defensive Efficiency Record, Established Performance Levels, Park Effects Charts, the Power-Speed Number, and many more. The formula for the Power-Speed Number, for instance, is $\frac{2(HR \times SB)}{HR + SB}$, and the highest single-season P-SN, James has found, belonged to Bobby Bonds in 1973, when he hit thirty-nine homers and stole forty-three bases for the Giants, for a P-SN of 40.9. But does anyone really *care* about this sort of thing? Sure they do: I do, for one.

Taken together, Sabermetrics and the Society for American Baseball Research and a book like Lawrence Ritter's *The Glory of Their Times* (a classic work of baseball reporting and history, in which great and obscure players of the first two decades of this century talk with affection and passion and humor about the old ball games) and all the other available serious reporting about baseball help explain one strange empty place, which is the shortage of good baseball novels. We have Ring Lardner's boobs and bushers, and Robert Coover's *The Great American Baseball Association*, and Bernard Malamud's *The Natural*, and Mark Harris's *The Southpaw* and *Bang the Drum Slowly*, but almost nothing else that I would put forward, even to another fan, as first-class fiction about our old pastime. Literature is better than sports, and one still wants an *Iliad* of our game, or a Huckleberry Finn in double-knit pinstripes, but I doubt that there is a Homer anywhere just now sitting down at his word processor and preparing to invent a league (with its teams, history, forefathers, dynasties, benevolent or bullying owners, legendary heroes, perpetual losers, nicknames, scandals, standings, box-scores, MVPs, and P-SN records) that can begin to do battle with the leagues and teams and players that we read about every morning in the newspapers—or hoping, for that matter, to make up a better Rollie

Fingers for us or to sketch in a John McGraw or a Willie Mc-Covey, a Babe Ruth or a Mark Fidrych, with sufficient art to make us *see* them, with absolute clarity, long after we have put down the book, or to dare to have his aging hero, Reggie Odysseus, conclude one episode of his hazardous summer journeys by winning the World Series with three successive monster home runs, struck with three swings of the bat. Who would believe *that*?

The exceptional baseball photographs that I have seen over the years must be beyond counting, but only a handful of them, I find, immediately come back to recollection. Willie Mays making his famous catch against Vic Wertz in the 1954 World Series, running full-tilt away from the plate and the camera (and helping us forever remember his number 24, across the back of his uniform), with the ball, in plain sight against the black screen of the Polo Grounds bleachers, about to drop like an egg into his open glove. . . . Ty Cobb sliding into third base in a swirl of dirt and vehemence; he is wearing a little striped cap, his jaw is clenched, and the force of his slide—he is already on the bag, safe once again—has knocked the third baseman's left foot up onto Cobb's left shoulder. . . . Judge Kenesaw Mountain Landis, the first commissioner, exuding probity and vision as he stares off into the middle distance, with his iron chin resting on the iron railing of his front-row box seat. . . . Babe Ruth absolutely surrounded with overjoyed youngsters in caps on some side street in the early 1920s; everybody is grinning and staring at the camera, and the Babe, in the exact center of the picture, is wearing a jaunty summer straw hat, a little bow tie, and the biggest grin of all. . . . Jackie

Robinson stealing home, with his extended right toe delicately aiming for the outermost sliver of the plate and the rest of his body, airborne, falling away from the lunging catcher (there are several such photos, in fact, taken at different times and in different games, but they are so much alike that they can almost be superimposed upon each other to make one sliding, thrilling Jackie Robinson—the picture that I see in my mind's eye). . . . Joe Rudi frozen mid-leap against the left-field fence with his glove outstretched above him to pull in a long clout in the 1972 World Series, and with the silhouette of his long body and reaching left arm and outstretched glove perfectly doubled in shadow on the wall beside him. . . . Lou Gehrig and Jimmy Foxx and Babe Ruth posing together for some photographer at Shibe Park in the late 1920s or early 1930s. They are in uniform, with Foxx in the middle (in his white home uniform, with the big, old-fashioned capital "A" over his heart), leaning against a low grandstand fence, with their spiked feet identically crossed. Their smiles and their easy, muscular affability suggest fame and danger and shared admiration: seventeen hundred and forty-one lifetime home runs saying hello.

There are other equally stirring photographs I could bring back to mind, I suppose, but it would take concentration. I have sometimes wondered why I should carry such a sparse gallery of baseball pictures with me after all these years, and I have simply attributed it to the built-in limitations of the medium, which must somehow squeeze this capacious, deeply three-dimensional sport (the struck ball bounding along on the outfield grass toward the oncoming center fielder, while, closer in, the sprinting base-runner starts his leaning turn around third base, as we in the stands—already measuring in our minds the distance of the hit against the distance from third to home, and factoring in the runner's speed against our knowledge of the fielder's arm—rise and hold our breath as we prepare to yell over the outcome of the crucial equation) into another eight-by-ten. It has dawned on me now, very late in the day, that I have unfairly held the same expectations of baseball photographers that I have of baseball novelists. I want them to capture the whole thing—the game and its history, the play and the pitch and the time of day, the noise of the crowd, and the look of the late-afternoon shadows darkening the stands along third base and beyond, and what I know about this particular pitcher and that batter and the man racing for the plate, and about this game and this season in which the play is taking place—and to put it all on the page for me, so that this fragment of baseball will always be mine, in perfect focus and understanding. It can't be done, of course, and once we understand that, there is a special pleasure in it and even a kind of relief, for we have sensed again the great ranges of variety and difficulty in the game, and the depth of our accompanying accumulated expertise and layered baseball emotions. We have also learned how to look at the wonderful photographs in this book.

Walter Iooss is a professional sports photographer, much admired in his demanding trade. He is a familiar sight at the game: a tall, cheerful photog in narrow jeans, with a trim beard and easy smile. Still a young man—he is just forty—he has been photographing football and basketball and baseball for more than twenty years now, mostly for *Sports Illustrated*. Someone else will have to say what Mr. Iooss knows about those other games, and still another expert will be required to talk about the technical side of his work. I know two things about him for a certainty: he knows a great deal about baseball, and he is a baseball fan. These attributes are not always interchangeable, by the way, but when they coexist in the same person, you have found yourself a terrific seatmate at the game. Walter Iooss is quick, of course— there are no laggards in his line of work—but he is also patient

page 77

page 59

page 62

page 122

and contemplative and involved. He has time for the quiet stretches of this pastime and for its rituals and preambles. His gaze takes in the silhouetted flags about the stands in the darkening evening sky, and then the hands of the kid (with bitten fingernails) holding a pen and a new ball at the ready as he hovers in wait for the next, best-ever autograph. Here is an early-bird fan all alone in the beautiful shiny green stands (it must be Fenway Park again), with his bare legs comfortably up on the seats below him, here in time to see *all* of batting practice for once. At spring training, Iooss keeps showing us the right part of the scenery—the modest, encompassing shot that conveys the news and the special feeling of this sweet part of the baseball year: the warm, cloud-filled blue air above the batting cage; the early-March light and shadow on Yogi Berra's face as he takes the sun and takes in his young hurlers and batters from his comfortable perch behind the netting; the little scattering of Cardinals not exactly killing themselves with work during their situps on the grass.

At the game, Iooss is avid and aware. He points, pokes your elbow, makes you notice. *Hey, did you see that? . . . Look how he's throwing. . . . Good play, good play. . . . Watch, he's going on this pitch. . . . I don't* believe *it!* You learn from him. The colors and gestures and meanings of baseball flow over you. You're in the game, as they say. (The games and the athletes on these pages have a particular value, by the way, since they illustrate that timeless feeling of baseball, once the action has begun, that I have mentioned. Players from different decades appear on the same or opposite pages, and yet each is playing the same game, beyond time and date.)

Two classic photographs here seem to belong on facing portals at Cooperstown. Bob Gibson, long and loose and in a hurry, is just beginning his windup, and, over on the other side, to your left, Harmon Killebrew is just completing a prodigious full cut at

page 112

page 68

page 58

page 87

the pitch, with his thick arms and back-leaning body and powerful legs all coming together on the fulcrum of the swing, and the ball—by the look of things—on its way toward the outermost sector of the bleachers. (You're paying attention if you've noticed that the textures of light and the look of the bunting and the crowd are very much the same in both pictures, for both were taken during the All-Star Game of 1965, in Minnesota. Killebrew, a home-town favorite, hit a two-run homer for the American League in the fifth inning—the picture has caught him hitting it—but not against Bob Gibson. The National League won the game, 6–5, and Gibson was credited with a save. A good day for both heroes, then, but not quite as good as Walter Iooss's, perhaps.)

page 76

Not all these photographs of pitchers and batters look like something struck for a medallion, but they can still show us how the game is played. Sandy Koufax is in mid-stride on the mound, with the acute angle of the small of his back forming an amazing arrow that is about to intersect the curved bow of his abdomen and trailing leg. It is a compelling silhouette, but there is more to it than aesthetics. Walter Iooss is telling us what we should know about Koufax—that it was his long back and lithe, sleekly muscled upper body that accounted for his devouring fastball and killing, down-darting curve during that brilliant stretch of years in the early sixties when his strikeout totals regularly exceeded his innings-pitched as he established himself, in many minds, at least, as the prime pitcher of our era. If we look at another picture of Bob Gibson, we can spot one source of *his* devastating heat in that characteristic running sidewise leap off the mound just after he released the ball. Almost the last of the old dominators, who counted fear as part of their repertoire, Gibson did not hesitate to knock down or plunk batters who had earned his displeasure, sometimes merely by the way they had swung at his previous

page 86

page 87

page 105

page 117

page 140

page 142

pitch. I once wrote a monograph about Gibson in which I commented at considerable length on these and other evidences of his unquenchable desire, but Walter Iooss has said it as well, and much more quickly, in the picture on page 87. The ball has just arrived in the catcher's upflung mitt, the batter (it is Don Demeter) is headed for the dirt, having thrown himself frantically away from the chin-high knockdown pitch, and Gibson—look at his face!—is once again in the exact center of everyone's attention.

The same sort of useful lessons are conveyed in most of these game photographs. The glowering Don Drysdale's eagle-wing sidearm style is nothing like Juan Marichal's celebrated over-the-top delivery, during which he kicks his front leg up higher than his head in midpitch, but in each case the difficult, telling mannerism is what works for that man and what helps set him so far above the lesser practitioners of his own trade. Look at Nolan Ryan's beautifully balanced and organized posture as he cocks and strides in preparation for another ninety-five m.p.h., and compare it with the wrenching after-pitch jump and stagger of athletes like Jim Bouton (his cap is on the ground, of course) and Steve Blass, who also got the job done but had to make desire do for elegance, and then please observe also the milder, less frantic demeanor of Tommy John, who habitually tantalizes and outmaneuvers the hitters, instead of just blowing them away.

Iooss's same curatorial touch reminds us of what we know or ought to know about the hitters, too—Carl Yastrzemski's body-lean and little forward half-stride into the pitch (were I a better curator I would be able to tell you the year and almost the month of this photograph, based on the degrees off-center of Captain Carl's stance—an angle he honed and fiddled with all through his twenty-three years at the plate); Willie Stargell's aristocratic cut at the ball, which always concluded with the bat gently drooping out of his right hand and with his body, facing the field now,

page 111

page 148

page 116

page 100

pages 84–85

pages 8–9

page 64

page 132

rising out of its butter-smooth circular swing. And so forth. Frank Robinson, who won a Most Valuable Player award in both leagues, stood closer to the plate than anyone else and could still muscle terrifying line drives into left field. How did he do that? With a top hand—the top forearm, really; look at the picture—that was quick enough and strong enough to turn over his wrists and pull the bat through an inside or outside pitch with equal speed and violence. Roberto Clemente, by perfect contrast, kept his bat back and *waited*—that beautiful, inside-out swing that placed the whole length of the bat on the same plane with the arriving pitch (in the picture, Clemente's wrists are moving the bat so swiftly that it outspeeds Iooss's camera-shutter) and could bonk an excellent in-on-the-hands pitch into the farthest corner of right field: another triple.

As I have suggested earlier, the repeated patterns of baseball satisfy us because they are at once familiar and unique. Every movement on the field reminds us of the same play, the same pitch, seen a thousand or fifty thousand times before, yet it is also new and of this moment, and has never been done exactly the way this player does it. Bob Bailey (a rookie here) snatches up a grounder at third and starts the peg over to second, and the dynamic line of his angled back leg and driving body flies upward into the umpire's dark and upright shape and then along the ump's pointing arm (he is signalling fair ball) and on out of the picture and page, on the same path as the coming peg. Giotto could not make it better. Brooks Robinson, seen between the legs of the batter as he races to first, closes in on a grounder (the ball is in line with his left shin in the picture) in a photograph that is made up of multiple triangles, but after I have admired the composition of the picture and have taken in the burning concentration of Robinson's gaze, I realize that the Iooss camera has also accentuated the other crucial baseball ingredient. What we finally noticed

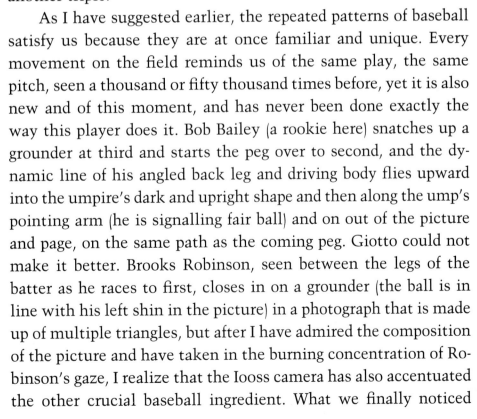

page 91

about Brooksie, I now remember, was not just his desire or his quickness and range but the delicacy of his touch—the almost feminine way his hands and arms found the ball (he is ambidextrous) and then collected it. "He can pick it" is the ballplayers' phrase for this sort of infield play, and I somehow think it must have been said first about Brooks Robinson.

page 147

page 158

page 132

page 107

Baseball is an extended family for its true fans, and there is a comfortable family-album aspect to Walter Iooss's work, as well. Here is Casey Stengel, a patriarch, scowling at the million accidents of the game and thinking of the next move (and the one after that) to stave off disaster once again. Here is the trim and noble Joe DiMaggio, in uniform for another old-timers' game, holding court in the clubhouse in his ancient robes of office. Here is Reggie Jackson once again saying something surprising and useful to a reporter (Reggie is a Hall of Fame interview, almost every time); and Pops Stargell, massively at his ease; and Yogi looking cheerful and gentle and, come to think of it, rather like something reflected in a hubcap; and Willie Mays, autographing baseballs, caught at a moment somewhere between the boyish sweetness of his first years in baseball and the bitter misanthropy of his last seasons (you can see both sides in the picture). There is a pervasive sadness here that we almost always feel when we look at old snapshots. Did Pete Rose ever wear his hair like *that*, and could he or any of us have guessed back then all the years and base hits that lay ahead—and that are now suddenly almost all gone by? Turn a page and there is Billy Martin ten years and four jobs ago (he was managing the Texas Rangers), before his demons had

page 160

page 143

page 134

page 93

turned him haggard. Mike Schmidt—thick red hair, that muscular clear gaze—looks like no one else in the world, but how many years will have to go by before this close-up, seen again, suddenly makes us think, How *young* he was! The sense of loss and later knowledge in these portraits should not surprise us, however, because this changing and aging and passing is one of the real purposes and attractions of professional sports. Teams are always young, always the same age, and yet with the passing of each season we can see players whom we know and care about growing visibly older and slower and nearer the end of their playing days; a career, a whole life on the field, lasts scarcely more than a decade and a half, and in that time we can watch the birth and boyhood and full maturity and middle age and approaching death of a man being played out, nobly or indifferently or badly, before our vicarious gaze.

page 62

We ask a lot of our athletes, I think. They are very well paid now, but what we expect of them is not just extraordinary skill but an intensity of effort and desire, day after day, that is probably greater than anything we will ask of ourselves in a year. When you look closely at the action photographs in this book, you see young men strained to the breaking point, burdened with pressure and mischance. The pitchers in mid-delivery are grimacing with the sudden violence of their efforts—and perhaps with pain, too. (In their minds always is an image like the one on page 138: Steve Busby, once a young star pitcher with the Kansas City Royals, sits in ice and bandages after another hard day in the minors, where he has been laboring—all in vain, it turned out—to restore his damaged arm to some semblance of health.) Everyday baseball happenings, caught in mid-instant, are excruciating. Joe Morgan, breaking for second base on a pickoff (it is the World Series of 1972) looks clenched and squeezed-down by the force of his muscles; Johnny Bench, out on a called third strike in the same Series,

page 138

page 120

page 145

Opposite: Little League. East Orange, New Jersey, June 1965

page 144

page 157

pages 2–3

page 115

page 156

sags with dejection and disbelief; Dave Concepcion, the shortstop, and Ivan DeJesus, the baserunner, lie in the dust together at second with identical looks and postures of pleading as they await the ump's call. At home plate (now we are in the late stages of the 1967 American League campaign), George Scott has just beaten the throw and scored a big run, and the grim, exhausted looks on the face of pitcher Jim Perry (behind the ump) and catcher Earl Battey tell us that this crucially important game and this season are not going to turn out right for the Twins, after all. Even the release of victory has something frantic and violent about it, because of the intensity of what has come just before. The writers shove and shout under the hot camera lights in the clubhouse, the winning players must run for their lives from the half-crazed fans (that's Jim Lonborg, with his uniform half torn off, being saved from the Fenway multitudes after his last-day, pennant-winning victory in 1967), and even the players' own World Series victory celebrations look more like a fight than a party. We want all this, of course, because we so badly need to care and to belong, but the price of such gifts comes high.

I think I prefer baseball's beginnings or middles to its great October resolutions. Every game, no matter how trifling, promises wonders, and we come to the park in mid-July feeling like children again, alight with hope. On this night, at Milwaukee's County Stadium (on pages 2–3), we have actually arrived a few minutes late—in the bottom of the first—but nothing has been lost. The midsummer sky still holds the last tints of day, but the floodlights are on, turning the outfield grass to emerald, and a quick look at the scoreboard tells us that the visiting Twins did nothing in the top of the inning. Our leadoff man has gotten to first already, and now there is a sudden shout and, by the look of things, more good news in the making.

Let's take our seats.

Little League. East Orange, June 1965

Left and opposite: Three-Quarter Century League Softball, St. Petersburg, Florida, April 1973

Girls' Softball. Pella, Iowa, September 1976

City Softball. Central Park, New York, November 1976

The Knothole Gang. Philadelphia Phillies Training Complex, Jack Russell Stadium,
Clearwater, Florida, March 1974

Spring Training. New York Mets, Al Lang Field, St. Petersburg, March 1969

Sam McDowell. Pittsburgh Pirates Training Complex, McKechnie Field, Bradenton, Florida, March 1974

Los Angeles Dodgers Training Camp. Dodgertown, Vero Beach, Florida, March 1983

Spring Training. Baltimore Orioles, Miami Stadium, Miami, March 1969

Dave Winfield. Fort Lauderdale Stadium, Fort Lauderdale, March 1981

Tom Seaver. Al Lopez Field, Tampa, March 1981

Pittsburgh Pirates Training Complex. April 1974

Rookie Pitcher. Holman Field, Dodgertown, March 1975

Dave Parker and Grant Jackson. McKechnie Field, March 1980

Red Schoendienst. St. Louis Cardinals Training Complex, St. Petersburg, March 1981

Dave Bristol. Al Lopez Field, March 1969

Yogi Berra. Huggins-Stengel Field, St. Petersburg, March 1975

Above and opposite: New York Mets Spring Training, Huggins-Stengel Field

Gene Mauch. Marchant Stadium, Lakeland, Florida, March 1975

Bernie Carbo. Al Lang Field, March 1980

Chuck Tanner. Sarasota, March 1975

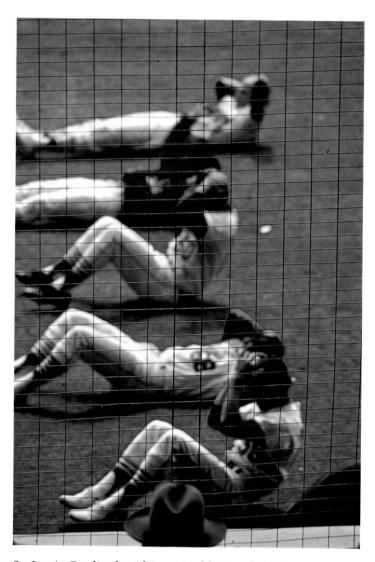

Bo Belinsky. Al Lang Field, March 1969

St. Louis Cardinals. Al Lang Field, March 1969

Mike Schmidt. Philadelphia Phillies Training Complex, March 1975

Security Guard. Al Lang Field, March 1980

Bob Bailey. McKechnie Field, March 1963

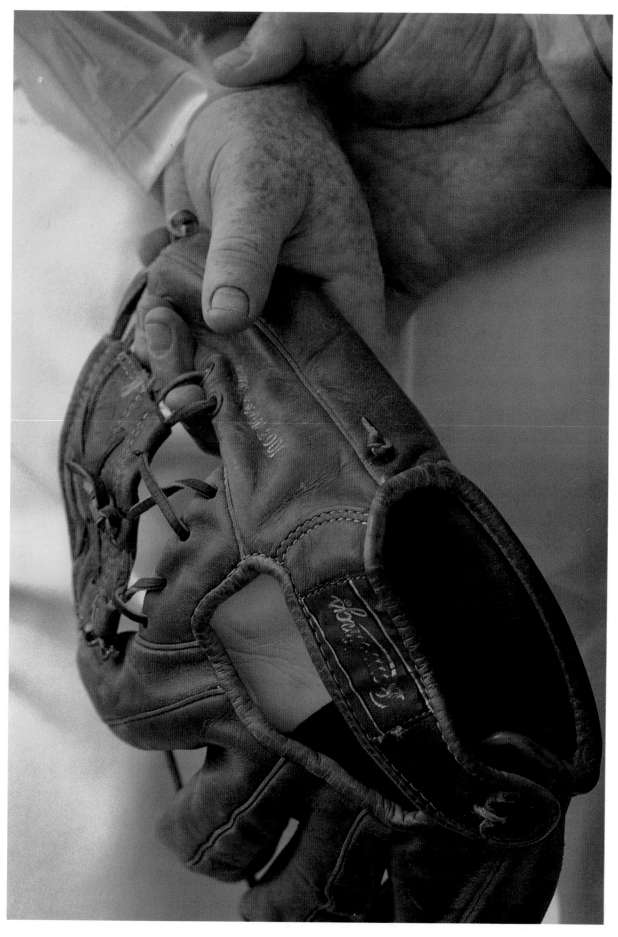

Red Schoendienst's Glove. Al Lang Field, March 1975

Following pages: Yankees. Miami Stadium, April 1981

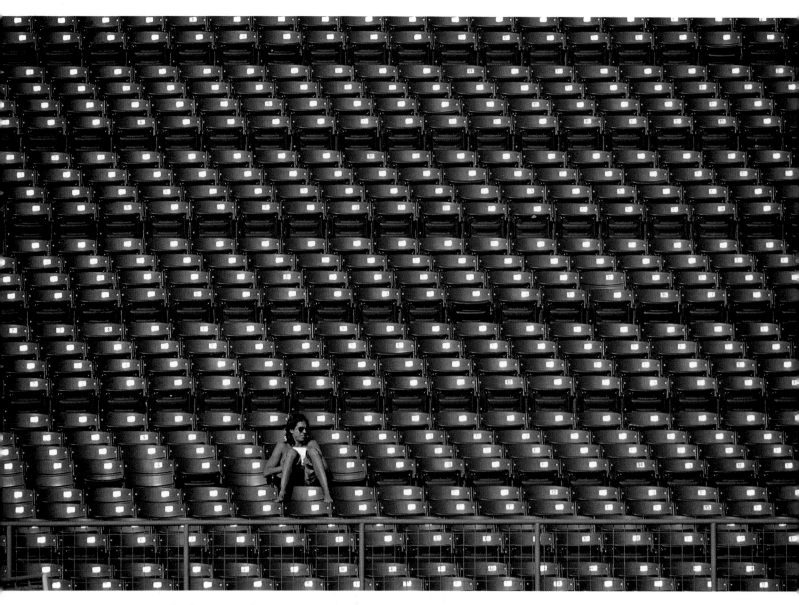

Fan. Fenway Park, August 1979

Opposite: Holman Field. Dodgertown. March 1982

Following pages: Six O'Clock Hitters. Arlington, Texas, June 1979

Dick Williams, Riverfront Stadium, World Series 1972

County Stadium. June 1979

Following pages: Walt Hrneak. Fenway Park, June 1979

Opposite: Sandy Koufax. Connie Mack Stadium, September 1964

Ken McKenzie. Jarry Park, May 1969

Cesar Cedeno. Dodger Stadium, Los Angeles, July 1972

Ed Figueroa and Catfish Hunter. Yankee Stadium, September 1976

Earl Weaver. Memorial Stadium, Baltimore, June 1974

Pittsburgh Fan. Forbes Field, Pittsburgh, 1963

Emmet Ashford and Fellow Umpires. Tiger Stadium, Detroit, World Series 1968

Kent Tekulve. Olympic Stadium, Montreal, April 1979

Randy Lerch. Dodger Stadium, July 1979

Sparky Anderson. Tampa, March 1975

Following pages: Frank Robinson. Memorial Stadium, 1968

Bob Gibson. Busch Stadium, St. Louis, August 1972.

Bob Gibson and Don Demeter. Connie Mack
Stadium, July 1962

Bruce Bochte. Fenway Park, August 1979

Ron Guidry. Dodger Stadium, World Series 1981

Roger Maris. Yankee Stadium, October 1962

Brooks Robinson. Tiger Stadium, July 1967

Johnny Bench. Riverfront Stadium, April 1974

Billy Martin. Municipal Stadium, Pompano Beach, March 1975

Following pages: Mickey Mantle. Municipal Stadium, April 1964

Mike Torrez. Connie Mack Stadium, August 1970

Jerry Koosman. Jarry Park, June 1969

Yaz. Fenway Park, August 1967

Tony Oliva. Fenway Park, September 1967

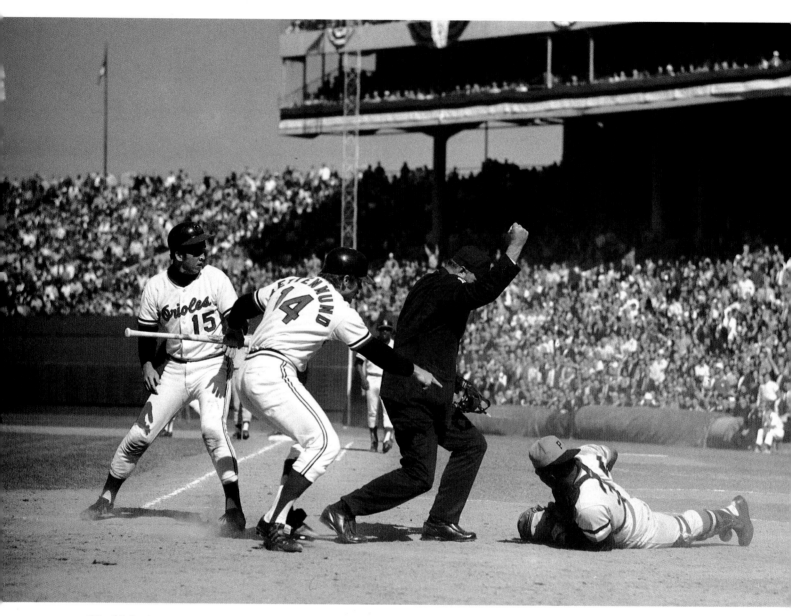

World Series Action. Memorial Stadium, October 1971

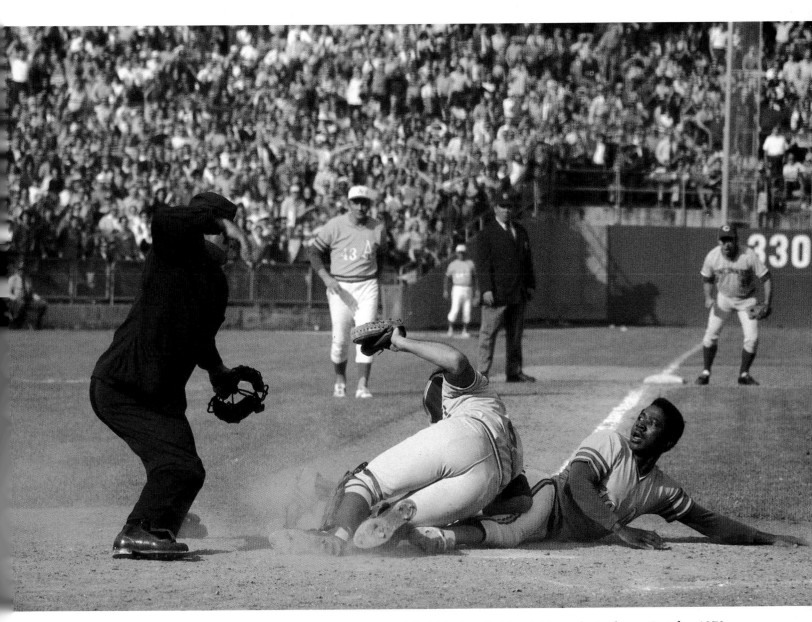

World Series. Oakland-Alameda Stadium, October 1972

Del Crandall (*left*) and Juan Marichal. Connie Mack Stadium, August 1965

Juan Marichal. Connie Mack Stadium, August 1965

Henry Aaron. West Palm Beach, Florida, April 1974

Pete Rose. Wrigley Field, Chicago, July 1964

Dick Allen. Comiskey Park Locker Room, Chicago, July 1972

Dick Allen. Holman Field, March 1971

Steve Carlton. Veterans Stadium, Philadelphia, 1980

Don Drysdale. Connie Mack Stadium, July 1965

Autograph Please. Fenway Park, August 1979

Yaz—Fielding. Fenway Park, August 1979

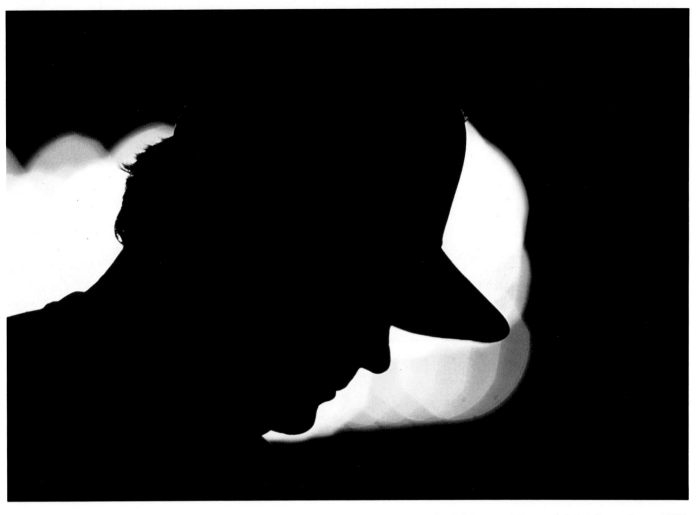

Earl Weaver. Memorial Stadium, June 1979

Don Zimmer. Fenway Park, August 1979

Al Kaline *(center)*. Tiger Stadium, May 1967

George Scott (left), Jim Perry (center), Earl Battey (right). Fenway Park, September 1967

Steve Blass. Memorial Stadium, World Series 1971

Jim Bouton. Metropolitan Stadium, August 1965

Pete Rose. Riverfront Stadium, World Series, 1972

Adolpho Phillips. Wrigley Field, July 1968

Joe Morgan, Riverfront Stadium, World Series 1972

Stolen Base—Maury Wills. Connie Mack Stadium, August 1965

Roberto Clemente. Forbes Field, Pittsburgh, July 1966

Gene Mauch. Connie Mack Stadium, June 1964

Opposite: Blue Moon Odom. Riverfront Stadium, World Series 1972

Goose Gossage. Yankee Stadium Equipment Room, August 1980

Reggie Jackson. Yankee Stadium Equipment Room, August 1980

Earl Wilson. Tiger Stadium, Detroit, May 1967

Ron Guidry. Yankee Stadium Equipment Room, August 1980

Following pages: Play at the Plate—Julian Javier. Fenway Park, October 1967

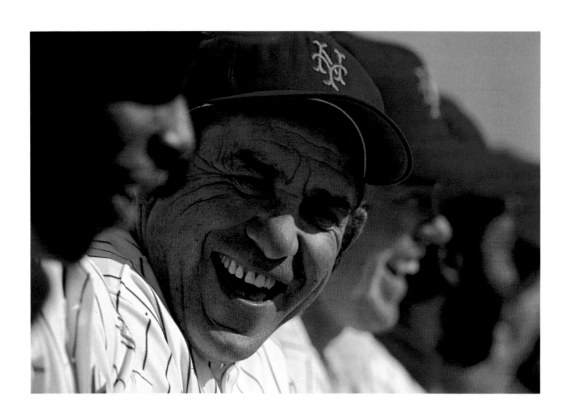

Vida Blue. Candlestick Park, San Francisco, May 1978

Opposite above: Yogi Berra. Huggins-Stengel Field, March 1975

Opposite below: Frank Robinson. Tiger Stadium, July 1967

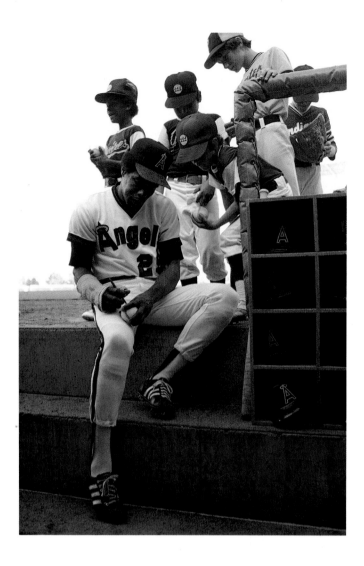

Rod Carew. Anaheim Stadium, Anaheim, July 1979

Willie Mays. County Stadium, September 1966

Under the Lights. Busch Stadium, July 1968

Following pages: Tony Scott and Garry Templeton. Dodger Stadium, June 1979

Steve Busby. Oklahoma City, June 1978

Ralph Houk. Marchant Stadium, March 1975

Tommy John. Metropolitan Stadium, June 1979

Opposite: Denny McLain. Tiger Stadium, World Series 1968

Willie Stargell. Three Rivers Stadium, August 1973

Willie Stargell. Olympic Stadium, August 1978

Dave Concepcion and Ivan DeJesus. Wrigley Field, June 1977

Johnny Bench. Oakland-Alameda Stadium, World Series 1972

Opposite: Clay Dalrymple, Art Mahaffey, Gene Mauch. Connie Mack Stadium, July 1963

Casey Stengel. Polo Grounds, Mets' first opening day, April 1962

Nolan Ryan. Anaheim Stadium, June 1979

Opposite: Frank Robinson. Memorial Stadium, World Series 1969

148

Following pages: Candlestick Park, July 1979

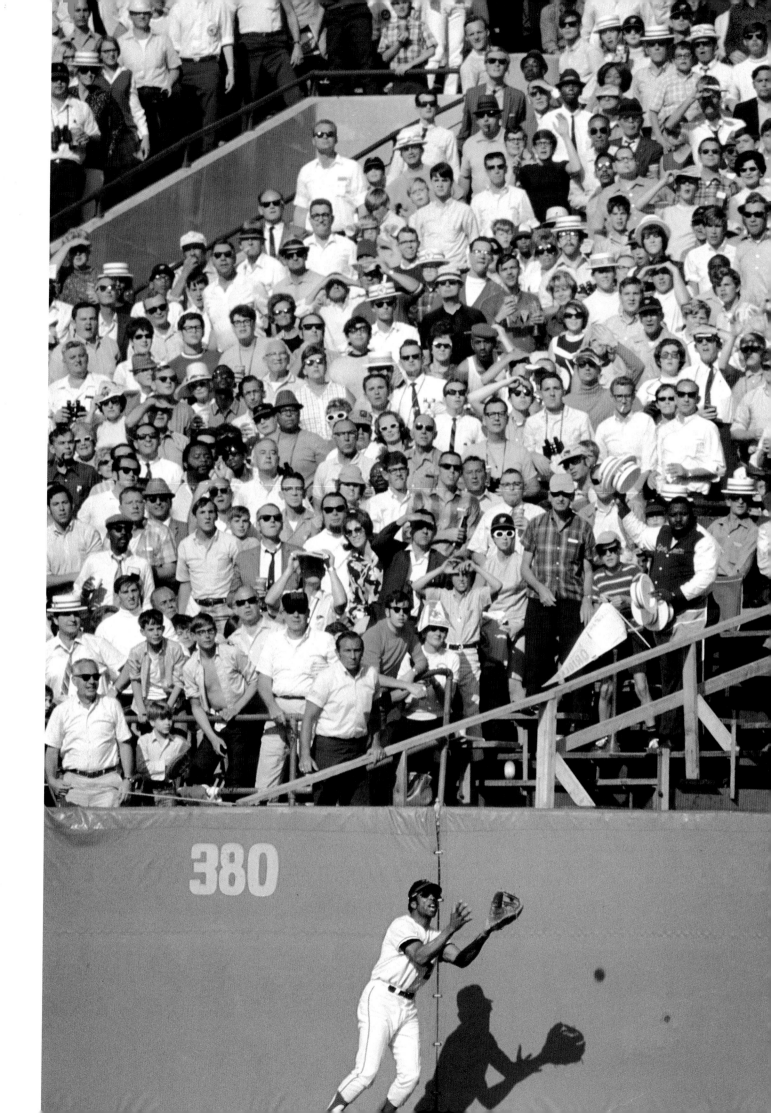

Tug McGraw. Royals Stadium, Kansas City, World Series 1980

Opposite: Tug McGraw. Astrodome, Houston, September 1980

Pirates Win Series. Memorial Stadium, October 1971

Series Win for Koufax. Yankee Stadium, October 1963

A's Win Series. Oakland-Alameda Stadium, October 1973

Opposite: Jim Lonborg—Pennant-Clinching Celebration. Fenway Park, September 1967

Reggie Jackson—Yanks Win Series. Yankee Stadium, October 1977

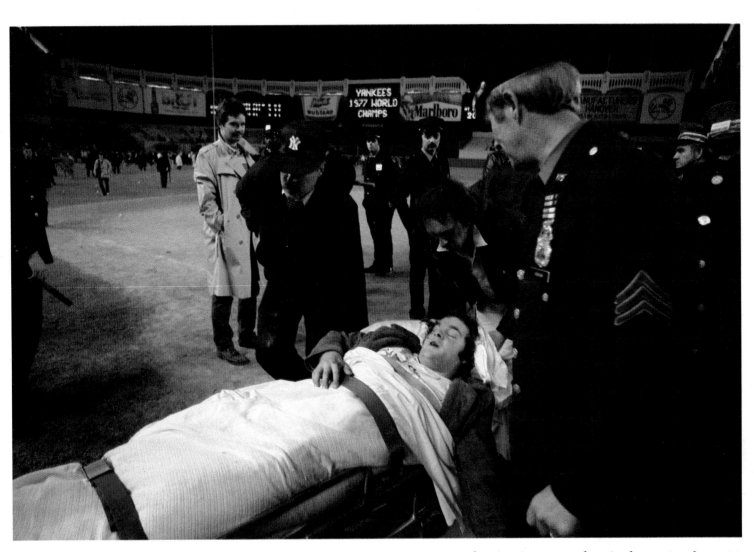

Fan—Yanks Win Series. Yankee Stadium, October 1977

Joe DiMaggio. Yankee Stadium Locker Room, Old Timers' Day, July 1979